やさしい英語で読む
グリム童話

Contents

目次

本書の利用法
06

長靴を はいたネコ *Puss in Boots*
08

ヘンゼルと グレーテル *Hansel and Gretel*
16

ハーメルンの 笛吹き *The Pied Piper*
24

ラプンツェル
Rapunzel
32

ブレーメンの音楽隊
The Musicians of Bremen — 40

白雪姫
Little Snow White — 48

赤ずきん
Little Red Riding Hood — 56

眠れる森の美女
Sleeping Beauty — 64

美女と野獣
Beauty and the Beast — 72

シンデレラ
Cinderella — 80

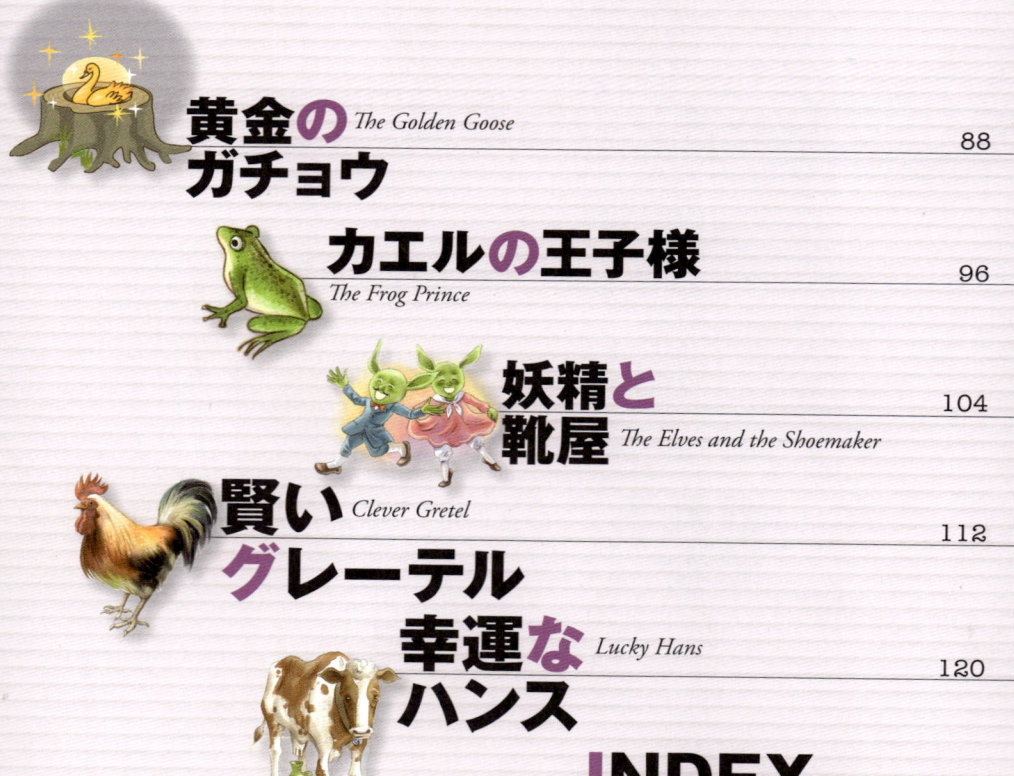

黄金のガチョウ *The Golden Goose* —— 88

カエルの王子様 *The Frog Prince* —— 96

妖精と靴屋 *The Elves and the Shoemaker* —— 104

賢いグレーテル *Clever Gretel* —— 112

幸運なハンス *Lucky Hans* —— 120

INDEX —— 128

学習法

本書を使って英語の読解力や聴解力をアップさせるのに有効な学習法を紹介します。
お話を楽しみながら、英語力を上げるのに役立ててください。

Step1
Vocabulary をヒントにしながら物語を読む

Step2
日本語訳で確認

Step3
CD（英語）を本を見ながら聞く

Step4
CD（英語）を本を見ないで聞く

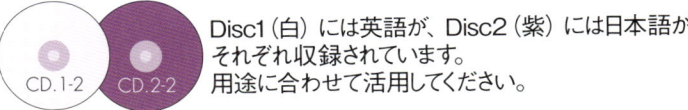

Disc1（白）には英語が、Disc2（紫）には日本語が
それぞれ収録されています。
用途に合わせて活用してください。

本書の利用法

CD.1-5

CDのトラック番号がここに示されています。CD1-5の場合は、Disc1（白）の"Track5"ということです。

Long ago, there was a very poor couple. They couldn't afford① food, so they took some vegetables from Dame Gothel's garden.

Dame Gothel saw this and got angry. She punished② the couple by taking their baby girl from them. She named her Rapunzel and kept her in a tall tower. The tower had no door and only one window at the top.

Years passed, and Rapunzel grew up to be a lovely woman with long hair. One day, a prince was nearby③

ここには、物語の中で使われている語彙を取り上げています。物語を読む際に、活用してください。

VOCABULARY

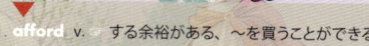
1. **afford** v. 〜する余裕がある、〜を買うことができる
2. **punish** v. 〜を罰する
3. **nearby** adj. すぐ近くの

品詞の表記について
n.　　　名詞
adj.　　形容詞
v.　　　動詞
v.aux.　助動詞
adv.　　副詞

Rapunzel ラプンツェル

▶ **本書は、誰もが知っているグリム童話 15 話を収録しています。
1 つのお話はイラストを含めて 8 ページで構成されており、
手軽に読み進めることができます。**

> CD のトラック番号がここに示されています。CD2-5 の場合は、Disc 2（紫）の "Track 5" ということです。

訳：ラプンツェル

CD.2-5

　昔々、とても貧しい夫婦がいました。2 人は食べ物さえ買うことができず、デイム・ゴーテルの庭から野菜をとってしまいました。

　デイム・ゴーテルはそれを見て怒り、罰として夫婦から女の子の赤ちゃんを取り上げました。ゴーテルはその子をラプンツェルと名付け、高い塔に閉じ込めました。塔には扉がなく、上に窓が 1 つあるだけでした。

　何年かが過ぎ、ラプンツェルは長い髪の美しい女性に成長しました。ある日、近くを訪れた王子が、ラプンツェルの歌声を耳にします。王子はすぐに恋に落ちました。

　王子は塔の入口を見つけることができません。そのときデイム・ゴーテルが来て、王子は隠れました。ゴーテルは叫びました。
「ラプンツェル！　髪を下ろすんだよ！」
ラプンツェルの髪が窓から下ろされ、デイム・ゴーテルはそれを使って塔を登っていきました。

ラプンツェル
Rapunzel

> 各お話の最後には日本語訳が見開きで載っています。日本語だけを読んでも自然なように、英語を意訳したものもありますので、必ずしも Vocabulary で紹介された意味と一致するとは限りません。

7

Puss in Boots
長靴を はいた ネコ

Once upon a time, an old miller died, and his possessions[1] were divided[2] among his three sons. The eldest son got the mill, and the second son got the donkey. Unfortunately, the youngest son was left with nothing but the miller's cat. Feeling disappointed,[3] the youngest son thought about getting rid of[4] the cat. However, the cat was clever and tried to bargain with[5] his new master. "Give me a bag and a pair of boots," the cat said, "and I will make you very rich."

The cat got his wish. Pulling on his new boots and throwing the bag over his shoulder, he went to a field where many rabbits lived. He caught some and presented them to the king as a gift from his master.

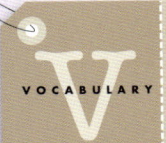

VOCABULARY
1. **possession** n. ☞ 財産
2. **divide** v. ☞ 分割する
3. **disappointed** adj. ☞ がっかりした
4. **get rid of** v. ☞ 追い払う
5. **bargain with~** v. ☞ 〜と駆け引きする

The king was very pleased.

Later on, the cat learned that the king would be traveling near a river. He told his master to bathe in the river. When the king and his beautiful daughter rode by, the cat stopped them and cried, "My master has been robbed❶ and is drowning!❷ Help him, please!"

The king saved the cat's master, dressed him in expensive clothes, and they rode off together. Meanwhile,❸ Puss raced ahead and met some farmers. Although the fields they were working in belonged to a powerful ogre,❹ he told the farmers say they belonged to his master. "If you don't," Puss threatened,❺ "I will beat you!" When the king arrived and asked who owned the fields, he heard the farmers say the young master's name.

1. **rob** v. ☞ 〜から奪う
2. **drown** v. ☞ 溺れ死ぬ
3. **meanwhile** adv. ☞ その一方で、その間
4. **ogre** n. ☞ 怪物
5. **threaten** v. ☞ 脅迫する

Puss in Boots 長靴をはいたネコ | 11

Puss was not finished. He met the ogre and started to flatter him. "Such a powerful ogre must have many talents,❶" the cat said. "I bet you can turn yourself into❷ anything, even a mouse!" To show the cat his skill, the ogre turned himself into a mouse. Puss then jumped on the mouse and ate it!

At last, Puss claimed❸ the ogre's land and castle for his master. When the king arrived, he was so impressed by the boy's wealth❹ that he asked Puss's master to marry his daughter, the princess. Thus, the youngest son of a poor miller became a prince thanks to the help of one cool cat, Puss in Boots.

VOCABULARY

1. **talent** n. ☞ 才能
2. **turn~ into…** v. ☞ ～を…に変化する
3. **claim** v. ☞ 獲得する
4. **wealth** n. ☞ 裕福

訳：長靴をはいたネコ

　昔々のこと。老いた粉引き職人が死に、3人の息子にその遺産が分けられました。長男は粉引き小屋、次男はロバをもらいました。不運なことに三男に残されたのは、粉引き職人の飼っていたネコだけ。がっかりした三男は、ネコを追い払おうと考えました。しかしネコは賢く、新しい主人と駆け引きをすることにします。
「私に袋と長靴をください」と猫は言いました。
「そうすれば、あなたを大金持ちにしましょう」

　猫の願いはかなえられました。新しい長靴をはき、袋を肩にかけると、ネコはたくさんのウサギがすむ野原に行きました。ウサギを何匹かつかまえると、主人からの贈り物として王様に差し出しました。王様はとても喜びました。

　その後、ネコは、王様が川の近くを訪れることを知ります。ネコは主人に川につかっているように言いました。王様とその美しい娘が馬に乗って通りかかると、ネコは2人を止めて泣き叫びました。
「私の主人が泥棒にあって溺れています！どうか助けてください！」

　王様はネコの主人を助け、高価な服を着せ、馬に乗って共に出発しました。この間、ネコは走って先回りし、農民たちに会いました。農民たちが働いて

いる野原は恐ろしい怪物が所有する土地でしたが、ネコは、自分の主人の土地だと言うように告げます。
「もし言わなかったら、やっつけちゃうぞ!」とネコは脅しました。到着した王様がこの野原は誰の持ち物かと問うと、農民たちは若い主人の名を言いました。

ネコの作戦はこれで終わりません。怪物に会うと、お世辞を言い始めました。
「こんなに強いあなたは、たくさんの才能をお持ちなのでしょう」とネコは言います。
「きっと何にでも変身することができることでしょう。ネズミにだって!」怪物は、ネコにその技を示すべく、ネズミに化けます。するとネコはネズミに飛びかかり食べてしまいました!

ついに、ネコは怪物の土地と城を主人のものにしたのです。到着した王様は、その裕福さに感服し、ネコの若き主人に、娘である王女と結婚してくれるよう頼みました。こうして1匹の賢いネコ、"長靴をはいたネコ"のおかげで、貧しい粉引き職人の三男は王子となったのでした。

Hansel and Gretel
ヘンゼルとグレーテル

Once upon a time, a poor woodcutter[1] lived in a small house in the woods. He had two children, Hansel and Gretel. He loved his son and daughter, but his second wife was mean[2] to them.

"There is not enough food," the wife said. "We have to get rid of the children!" He was sad, but he couldn't stand up to[3] her.

The woodcutter gave the children some bread and took them far in the woods. He left them alone. Hansel had made a trail of bread crumbs[4] from their

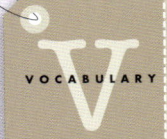

VOCABULARY

1. **woodcutter** n. ☞ きこり
2. **mean** adj. ☞ 意地悪な
3. **stand up to** v. ☞ 反抗する
4. **bread crumb** n. ☞ パンくず

Hansel and Gretel ヘンゼルとグレーテル

home. However, birds ate the crumbs. They were lost.

Hansel and Gretel stayed in the woods overnight. The next day, they looked for a way home. They came upon❶ a strange house made of candy. They were very hungry, so they broke off❷ pieces of the house and ate them.

Suddenly, the front door opened. An old woman looked out. "Come in!"❸ she said. "I have more candy for you."

Actually, the old woman was an evil witch!❹ She locked Hansel in a cage and forced Gretel to do housework.❺ She wanted to make Hansel fat before she ate him.

VOCABULARY

1. **come upon** v. ☞ ～に行き当たる
2. **break off** v. ☞ ちぎる
3. **come in** v. ☞ 中に入る
4. **witch** n. ☞ 魔女
5. **housework** n. ☞ 家事

Hansel and Gretel ヘンゼルとグレーテル

A few weeks later, the witch thought it was about time to eat Hansel. She told Gretel to light❶ the oven. "I don't know how!" Gretel lied.

"Foolish child! I'll do it," the witch said angrily. When she leaned into❷ the oven and lit up the fire, Gretel pushed her into the fire. She let Hansel out and took the witch's treasure.

The woodcutter was glad to see his children again. He told them their stepmother❸ had died. They had the witch's treasure and lived happily ever after.❹

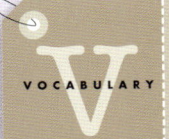

1. **light** v. (light-lit-lit) ☞ ～に火をつける
2. **lean into** v. ☞ 身を乗り出す
3. **stepmother** n. ☞ 継母
4. **live happily ever after** ☞ それからずっと幸せに暮らす

訳：ヘンゼルとグレーテル

　昔々、森の中の小さな家に貧しい木こりが暮らしていました。木こりには、ヘンゼルとグレーテルという２人の子供がいました。木こりはこの息子と娘を愛していましたが、木こりの後妻は２人にいじわるでした。

「食べ物が足りないわ」と妻は言いました。
「子供たちを追い出さないと！」
木こりは悲しみましたが、妻に反論することができません。

　木こりは子供たちにいくらかのパンを与え、森深くに連れて行き、置き去りにしました。ヘンゼルは、家からの道すがらパンくずを落として道しるべを作っておきました。ところが、鳥たちが食べてしまい、道に迷ってしまいます。

　ヘンゼルとグレーテルは森で一晩過ごしました。翌日、２人は家までの道を探しました。すると砂糖菓子で出来た不思議な家に出くわします。２人はとても空腹だったので、家のかけらをちぎって食べました。

　突然、玄関のドアが開き、老女が顔をのぞかせました。

「お入り!」と老女は言いました。
「もっとたくさんお菓子があるよ」

実は、この老女は邪悪な魔女だったのです!魔女はヘンゼルを檻の中に閉じ込め、グレーテルに家事をさせました。ヘンゼルを太らせて食べてしまおうとしたのです。

数週間後、魔女はそろそろヘンゼルの食べ頃だと考えました。魔女はグレーテルに、オーブンの火をつけるように言いました。
「やり方がわかりません!」とグレーテルは嘘をつきました。

「バカな子供だね!私がやるよ」
魔女は怒って言いました。魔女がオーブンにかがみ込んで火をつけたとき、グレーテルは魔女を火の中に押し込みます。グレーテルはヘンゼルを檻から出し、魔女の宝物を持ち出しました。

木こりは再び子供たちに会えて喜び、継母が死んだことを告げました。3人は魔女の宝物を得て、それからずっと幸せに暮らしました。

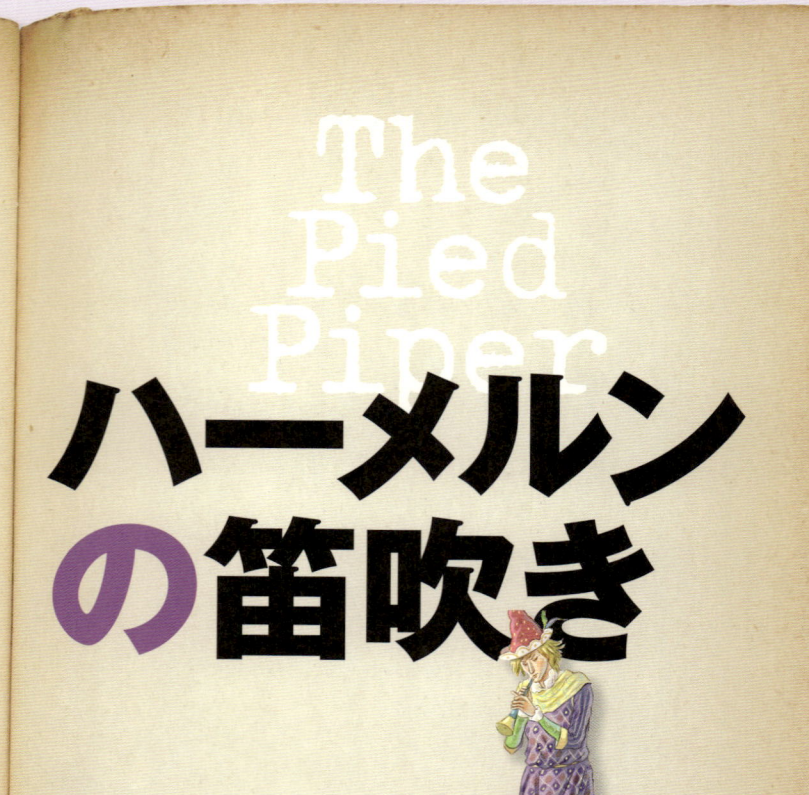

The Pied Piper
ハーメルンの笛吹き

Long ago, there was a small town called Hamelin. The town had a very big problem. It had hundreds of ❶ rats!

The townspeople❷ tried everything to get rid of them. However, nothing ever worked.

One day, a stranger❸ came to the town. "You may call me the Pied Piper," he said. "I am good at❹ catching rats, so I can help you." The people of the town were very happy to hear that. They promised to pay him well if he succeeded.❺

VOCABULARY

1. **hundreds of** ☞ 何百もの、ものすごい数の
2. **townspeople** n. ☞ 町の住人
3. **stranger** n. ☞ 見知らぬ人
4. **(be) good at** ☞ 〜が得意だ
5. **succeed** v. ☞ 成功する

The Pied Piper ハーメルンの笛吹き

The Pied Piper played his magic pipe. Soon, the rats in the town were attracted[1] by the music. As the Pied Piper walked, all the rats followed him.

He kept playing until he brought the rats into the river. Then all the rats drowned!

The townspeople cheered[2] when they found out. However, they did not pay the man as they promised. "We are pleased with your work, but we are very poor," they said. "We have no money to give you." The Pied Piper got very angry and left the town.

1. **attract** v. ☞ 引きつける
2. **cheer** v. ☞ 歓声を上げる

1. **in secret** ☞ 秘密に、こっそり
2. **lead** v. (lead-led-led) ☞ 先導する
3. **fee** n. ☞ 謝礼金
4. **fault** n. ☞ 責任、過ち

A week later, the Pied Piper returned to Hamelin in secret.❶ He played his pipe again. This time, he attracted the children of the town.

The children followed the sound of the music. The Pied Piper led❷ them far from the town. Then he sent a message to the townspeople. He said he would return the children, but he wanted to be paid twice his fee.❸

The townspeople had no choice but to pay him. "It's our fault❹ for not keeping our promise," they said. It was an expensive lesson to learn.

訳：ハーメルンの笛吹き

　昔々、ハーメルンという小さな町がありました。その町はとても大きな問題を抱えていました。ものすごい数のネズミがいたのです！

　町の人たちはネズミを駆除するためにあらゆる手を尽くしました。しかし何もうまくいきませんでした。

　ある日、見知らぬ者が町にやって来ました。「まだら服の笛吹き」と呼んでくれと、その男は言いました。
「僕はネズミ捕りが得意なんだ。だから、君たちを助けられるよ」
町の人々はそれを聞いてとても喜び、成功したらたくさんのお金を払うと約束しました。

　まだら服の笛吹きは魔法の笛を吹きました。すぐに町のネズミたちはその音色にひき寄せられました。まだら服の笛吹きが歩くと、ネズミたちがその後をついていきます。

　男は、ネズミを川の中に連れ込むまで吹き続けました。そして、ネズミはすべて溺れてしまいました。

町の人々は、それを知って大喜び。しかし、約束したお金は払いませんでした。
「あなたのしてくれたことはうれしいけど、私たちはとても貧しいのです」
と人々は言いました。
「あなたにあげるお金がありません」
まだら服の笛吹きはとても怒って、町を去ってしまいました。

　1週間後、まだら服の笛吹きはひそかにハーメルンに戻って来ました。男はまた笛を吹きました。今度は、町の子供たちをひき寄せました。

　子供たちはその音色についていきました。笛吹き男は子供たちを町から遠く離れた場所に連れていきました。そして町の人々にメッセージを送ったのです。「子供たちは帰すが、2倍の報酬を払ってほしい」と。

　町の人々は男に金を払うほかありません。
「約束を守らなかったのは私たちの過ちです」と人々は言いました。高い授業料となりました。

Rapunzel
ラプンツェル

Long ago, there was a very poor couple. They couldn't afford[1] food, so they took some vegetables from Dame Gothel's garden.

Dame Gothel saw this and got angry. She punished[2] the couple by taking their baby girl from them. She named her Rapunzel and kept her in a tall tower. The tower had no door and only one window at the top.

Years passed, and Rapunzel grew up to be a lovely woman with long hair. One day, a prince was nearby[3]

1. **afford** v. ☞ する余裕がある、〜を買うことができる
2. **punish** v. ☞ 〜を罰する
3. **nearby** adj. ☞ すぐ近くの

Rapunzel ラプンツェル

and heard Rapunzel singing. He immediately❶ fell in love with her.

The prince couldn't find the tower's entrance. Then, he hid because Dame Gothel was coming. She shouted, "Rapunzel! Let down your hair!" Rapunzel's long hair fell from the window, and Dame Gothel used it to climb into the tower.

After Dame Gothel left, the prince called Rapunzel's name. She let her hair down. A few minutes later, the handsome❷ prince was at her window. It was love at first sight.❸

Later that evening, the prince found a ladder and helped Rapunzel escape. However, Rapunzel wasn't free for long. Dame Gothel caught her.

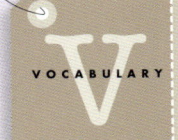

VOCABULARY

1. **immediately** adv. ☞ すぐに
2. **handsome** adj. ☞ ハンサムな、顔立ちの美しい
3. **at first sight** ☞ ひと目で

Dame Gothel was so angry that she cut off Rapunzel's hair. The prince tried stopping her but fell into❶ some bushes.❷ This blinded❸ him, and he couldn't see where Dame Gothel took Rapunzel.

He spent many years searching for Rapunzel. He would give anything to hear her voice again.

While searching the desert,❹ he heard a familiar voice singing. He found Rapunzel! She was so happy that she cried. When some of her tears fell into the prince's eyes, he could finally see again! Later, they got married and lived happily ever after.

VOCABULARY

1. **fall into** v. ☞ 〜に落ちる
2. **bush** n. ☞ 茂み
3. **blind** v. ☞ 〜を失明させる
4. **desert** n. ☞ 砂漠

訳：ラプンツェル

　昔々、とても貧しい夫婦がいました。2人は食べ物さえ買うことができず、デイム・ゴーテルの庭から野菜をとってしまいました。

　デイム・ゴーテルはそれを見て怒り、罰として夫婦から女の子の赤ちゃんを取り上げました。ゴーテルはその子をラプンツェルと名付け、高い塔に閉じ込めました。塔には扉がなく、上に窓が1つあるだけでした。

　何年かが過ぎ、ラプンツェルは長い髪の美しい女性に成長しました。ある日、近くを訪れた王子が、ラプンツェルの歌声を耳にします。王子はすぐに恋に落ちました。

　王子は塔の入口を見つけることができません。そのときデイム・ゴーテルが来て、王子は隠れました。ゴーテルは叫びました。
「ラプンツェル！髪を下ろすんだよ！」
ラプンツェルの髪が窓から下ろされ、デイム・ゴーテルはそれを使って塔を登っていきました。

　デイム・ゴーテルが去ると、王子はラプンツェルの名を呼びました。ラプ

ンツェルは髪を下ろします。数分後、顔立ちの美しい王子が窓に現れました。ひと目惚れでした。

その夜遅く、王子ははしごを見つけ、ラプンツェルの逃亡を手伝います。しかし、ラプンツェルは長く自由ではいられませんでした。デイム・ゴーテルにつかまってしまったのです。

デイム・ゴーテルは激怒し、ラプンツェルの髪を切ってしまいました。王子は止めようとしましたが、茂みの中に落ちてしまいます。そのために王子は失明し、デイム・ゴーテルがどこにラプンツェルを連れて行ってしまったかわからなくなってしまいました。

王子はラプンツェルを何年もかけて探しました。王子は、再びその声を聞くためなら何でもするつもりでした。

砂漠を探していると、王子は懐かしい歌声を耳にします。ラプンツェルを見つけたのです！ラプンツェルはうれしくて泣きました。その涙が王子の目に落ちると、ついに王子の目は再び見えるようになりました。その後、2人は結婚してずっと幸せに暮らしました。

The Musicians of Bremen
ブレーメンの音楽隊

Once upon a time, there was a hardworking donkey. He worked dutifully[1] and never complained.[2] However, his master planned to get rid of him because he was getting older and weaker. The donkey decided to run away[3] and become a musician in Bremen. Animals there enjoyed freedom and lived without owners.

On his way to Bremen, he met a dog that told him, "My owner is going to shoot me because I am too old to hunt." The donkey encouraged[4] him to escape and join his band, so they set off[5] together.

VOCABULARY

1. **dutifully** adv. ☞ うやうやしく
2. **complain** v. ☞ 文句を言う
3. **run away** v. ☞ 逃げる
4. **encourage** v. ☞ 勧める
5. **set off** v. ☞ 出発する

1. **capture** v. ☞ とらえる
2. **crow** v. ☞ （おんどりが）鳴く
3. **chop off** v. ☞ 切り落とす
4. **bray** v. ☞ いななく
5. **meow** v. ☞ ニャーと鳴く

Shortly after, they met an old cat. The cat's owner wanted to drown him because he was not fast enough to capture❶ mice anymore. The cat also agreed to join the music group. Later on a farm, they met a rooster crowing❷ at the top of his lungs. "I am singing my good-bye because tomorrow my owner will chop off❸ my head and eat me," said the rooster. "Cheer up. Use your beautiful voice to make music with us," the donkey suggested.

That evening, they saw a group of robbers having a big meal in a house. To earn some food, they performed their music. The donkey brayed,❹ the dog barked, the cat meowed,❺ and the rooster crowed. The terrible noise scared the robbers, and they ran into the forest.

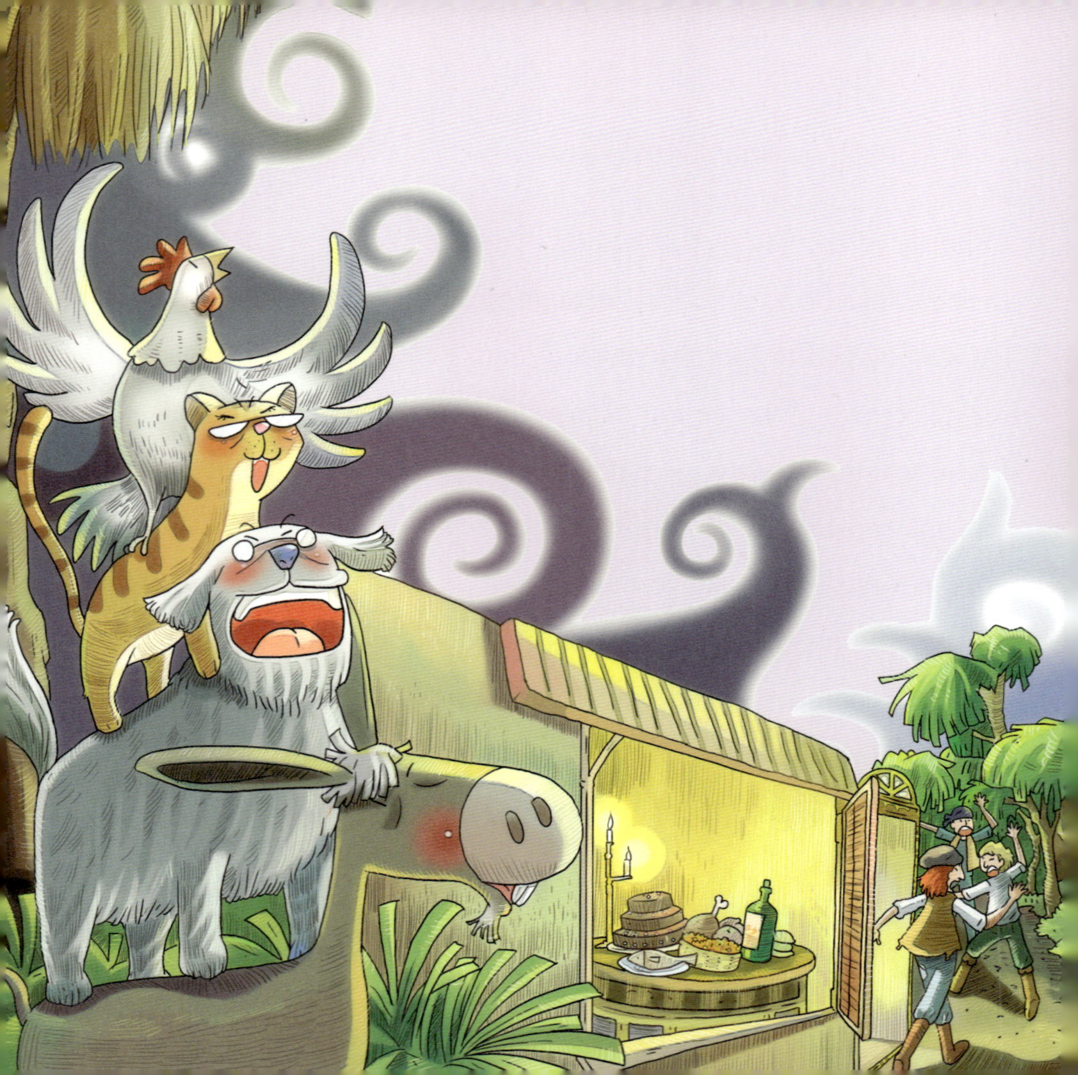

The animals went inside the house, ate, and went to bed. Later that night, one of the robbers returned. In the darkness, he mistook the cat's shining eyes for coals[1] and reached for them to light his candle. Suddenly, all of the animals attacked. The cat scratched him, the donkey kicked him, the dog bit him, and the rooster crowed and chased him away.

The robber told the others that a witch (the cat) cut him with long fingernails, and a man (the dog) stabbed[2] him with a sharp knife. Then a monster (the donkey) beat him with a club,[3] and a devil (the rooster) screamed[4] at him.

The frightened robbers dared[5] not go back to the house again. The animals took over the house and lived happily ever after.

VOCABULARY

1. **coal** n. ☞ 石炭
2. **stab** v. ☞ 〜を刺す
3. **club** n. ☞ こん棒
4. **scream** v. ☞ 鋭い叫び声を上げる
5. **dare** v.aux. ☞ あえて〜する

訳：ブレーメンの音楽隊

　昔々、働き者のロバがいました。ロバは文句も言わず律儀に働きました。しかし、主人は、ロバが年老いて体が弱くなってきたため、お払い箱にしようと考えました。ロバは脱走し、ブレーメンで音楽家になろうと心に決めます。そこでは、動物たちが自由を満喫し、飼い主に飼われることなく暮らしていました。

　ブレーメンへの道すがら、ロバはイヌに会いました。
「私の主人は、狩りをするには年をとりすぎているからと、私を撃とうとするのです」とイヌは言いました。ロバはイヌに、逃げて自分の音楽隊に加わるようにすすめ、一緒に出発しました。

　間もなく、2匹は年老いたネコに会いました。ネコの主人は、ネコの動きがのろくてこれ以上ネズミをつかまえられないからと、溺死させようとしていました。ネコも音楽隊に入ることに同意しました。しばらくすると、農場で声を限りに鳴いているおんどりに出会いました。
「明日、主人が私の首をはねて食べてしまうので、お別れの歌を歌っているのです」とおんどりは言いました。
「元気を出して。僕たちと音楽を奏でるためにその美しい声を使ってよ」
とロバは提案しました。

その夜、一行は、家でごちそうを食べている泥棒の一味を見つけます。食べ物を得るため、彼らは音楽を演奏しました。ロバが騒々しくいななき、イヌが吠え、ネコがニャーと鳴き、おんどりが雄叫びをあげました。そのひどい音に泥棒たちは震え上がり、森の中に逃げてしまいました。

　動物たちは家に入り、食べ、寝ました。その夜遅く、泥棒の1人が戻ってきました。暗闇の中、泥棒はネコの光る瞳を石炭と間違え、つかみとろうと、ろうそくに火を灯しました。すると突然、動物たちが皆で襲いかかりました。ネコがひっかき、ロバが蹴り、イヌが噛み付き、おんどりが鳴いて、追い払いました。

　泥棒はほかの仲間に、魔女（ネコ）が長い指のツメで切り付け、男（イヌ）が鋭いナイフで突き刺し、怪物（ロバ）がこん棒で打ち付け、悪魔（おんどり）が金切り声を浴びせたと言いました。

　おびえた泥棒たちは二度と家に戻ろうとはしませんでした。動物たちは家を乗っ取り、それからずっと幸せに暮らしました。

Little Snow White

白雪姫

Once upon a time, a queen died after giving birth to[1] a baby girl. The baby was as white as snow, so she was named Snow White.

A year later, the king married a woman who was beautiful but lacked goodness.[2] Every day, the new queen would look in her mirror and ask, "Mirror, mirror, on the wall, who's the fairest[3] of them all?" The mirror would always reply, "You, my queen."

However, as Snow White grew up, she became more and more lovely. One day, when the queen asked the mirror her question, the mirror replied,

VOCABULARY

1. **give birth to** v. ～を産む
2. **goodness** n. 親切さ、善良
3. **fair** adj. 美しい

Little Snow White 白雪姫

"Snow White is the fairest of them all." This filled the queen with anger.

The next day, the queen sent a servant ❶ to kill Snow White. Out of pity,❷ he set her free instead. Snow White wandered❸ the forest until she saw a little house.

The house belonged to seven dwarves.❹ "If I cook and do the housework, can I stay here?" Snow White asked. The dwarves happily agreed.

The evil queen soon discovered that Snow White was still alive. The queen dressed like an old peddler❺ and went to the dwarves' home. "Try a juicy apple," she told Snow White. Not knowing the apple was filled with poison, Snow White bit into it. Then she fell down dead!

VOCABULARY

1. **servant** n. 家来
2. **out of pity** 気の毒に思って
3. **wander** v. さまよう
4. **dwarf** n. 小人 ［複数形：dwarves］
5. **peddler** n. 行商人

Little Snow White 白雪姫

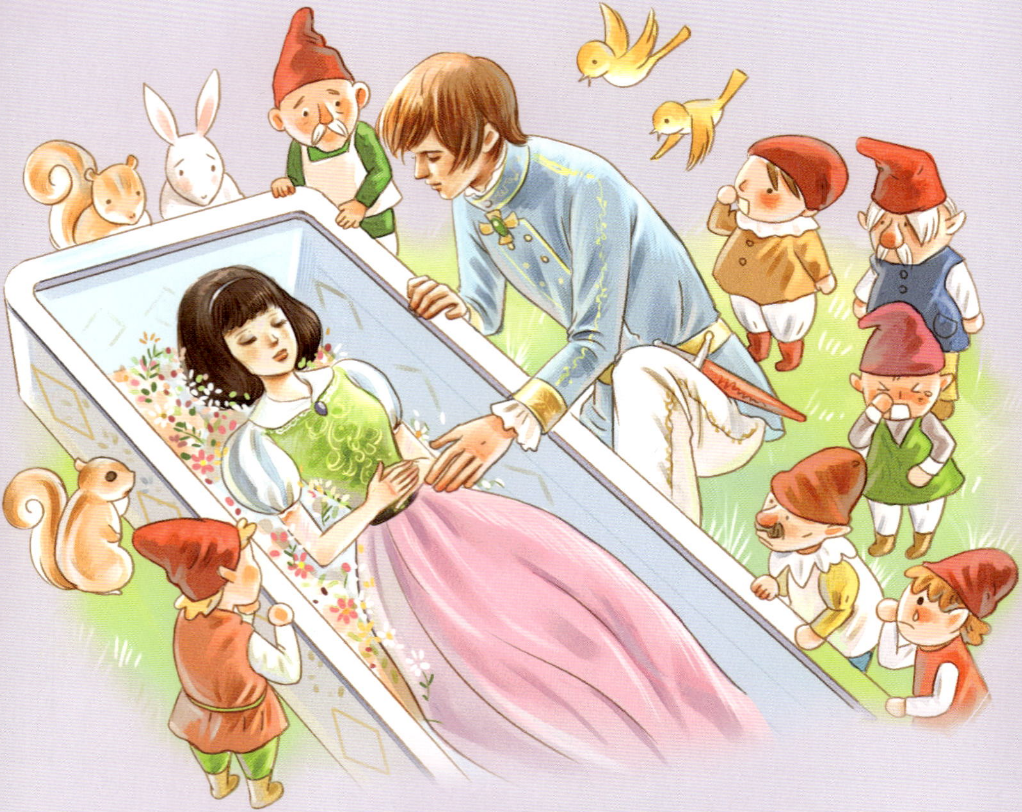

When the seven dwarves arrived home, they set eyes on[1] the dead princess. "Our poor Snow White!" they cried. With great sorrow,[2] they laid the princess in a glass coffin.[3]

As the dwarves were mourning[4] her, a prince rode by. The dwarves told the prince what happened and he felt sorry for Snow White. The prince kissed her, making the piece of poisoned apple fall from her lips. Snow White slowly began to wake. "She's alive!" cried the happy dwarves.

The prince soon married Snow White. All seven dwarves came to the wedding. And what happened to the awful[5] queen? She was forced to leave and was never heard from again.

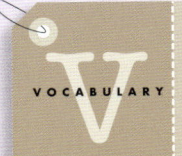

VOCABULARY

1. **set eyes on** v. ☞ ～を見る
2. **with great sorrow** ☞ 大きな悲しみをもって
3. **coffin** n. ☞ ひつぎ
4. **mourn** v. ☞ 嘆き悲しむ
5. **awful** adj. ☞ ひどい

訳：白雪姫

　昔々、お妃が、女の子の赤ちゃんを生んだ後、亡くなってしまいました。赤ちゃんは雪のように白かったので、白雪姫と名付けられました。

　1年後、王はある女性と結婚しました。その女性は、美しいけれども思いやりのない人でした。新しいお妃は、毎日、鏡をのぞき、たずねます。
「鏡よ、鏡よ、鏡さん。この世でいちばん美しいのは誰？」
鏡はいつも答えます。
「あなたです。お妃様」

　しかし、白雪姫は成長するにつれ、どんどん愛らしくなっていきました。ある日、お妃が鏡にいつもの質問をすると、鏡はこう答えたのです。
「白雪姫こそいちばん美しい」
お妃は怒りでいっぱいになりました。

　翌日、お妃は白雪姫を殺すために家来を送りました。かわいそうに思った家来は、白雪姫を逃がします。白雪姫は森をさまよい、小さな家を見つけました。

　家は7人の小人のものでした。
「私が料理と家事をすれば、ここにいてもいいかしら」
白雪姫がたずねると、小人たちは喜んで賛成しました。

悪魔のようなお妃は、白雪姫がまだ生きていることをすぐにかぎつけました。年老いた行商人の格好をしたお妃は、小人たちの家に行きます。
「みずみずしいリンゴはいかが」とお妃は白雪姫に言いました。
リンゴに毒が盛られていることを知らない白雪姫は、リンゴにかじりつきました。そして、倒れて死んでしまったのです！

　7人の小人は、家に帰ると、死んでしまった姫を目にします。
「かわいそうな白雪姫！」
小人たちは嘆き、たいそう悲しみながら、ガラスのひつぎに姫を横たえました。

　小人たちが悲しみにくれていると、馬に乗った王子が通りかかりました。小人たちは何が起きたかを話すと、王子は白雪姫に同情しました。王子が白雪姫にキスをすると、毒リンゴのかけらが姫の唇からポロリと落ちました。白雪姫はゆっくりと目を覚ましました。
「姫は生きている！」
喜んだ小人たちは叫びました。

　王子はすぐに白雪姫と結婚し、7人の小人たちは結婚式に出席しました。そして、あの恐ろしいお妃がどうなったかって？お妃は追放され、その後の消息はまったくわからないのです。

Little Red Riding Hood

赤ずきん

Once upon a time, there was a little girl who lived in the woods[1] with her mother. Her name was Little Red Riding Hood.

One day, her mother said to her, "Please take this basket of food to your grandmother. Go straight to her house and don't talk to strangers!"

"I promise," said Little Red Riding Hood, and she set off down the path.[2] After a few minutes, she saw a wolf.

"Where are you going, little girl?" asked the wolf.

VOCABULARY

1. **live in the woods** v. 森で暮らす
2. **path** n. 小道

Little Red Riding Hood 赤ずきん

Little Red Riding Hood forgot all about her promise and said, "I'm going to Granny's① house!"

The wolf quickly ran to Granny's house. He burst through② the door and locked Granny in the basement.③ Then he put on Granny's pajamas,④ got into her bed, and waited.

A few minutes later, Little Red Riding Hood arrived. She was surprised that Granny looked so different! "What big eyes you have, Granny!" she said.

"The better to see you with," said the wolf.

"And what big teeth you have!"

"The better to eat you with!" shouted the wolf. And he jumped out of

VOCABULARY

1. **granny** n. ☞ おばあちゃん
2. **burst through** v. ☞ ～から突然現れる
3. **basement** n. ☞ 地下室
4. **pajamas** n. ☞ パジャマ

Little Red Riding Hood 赤ずきん

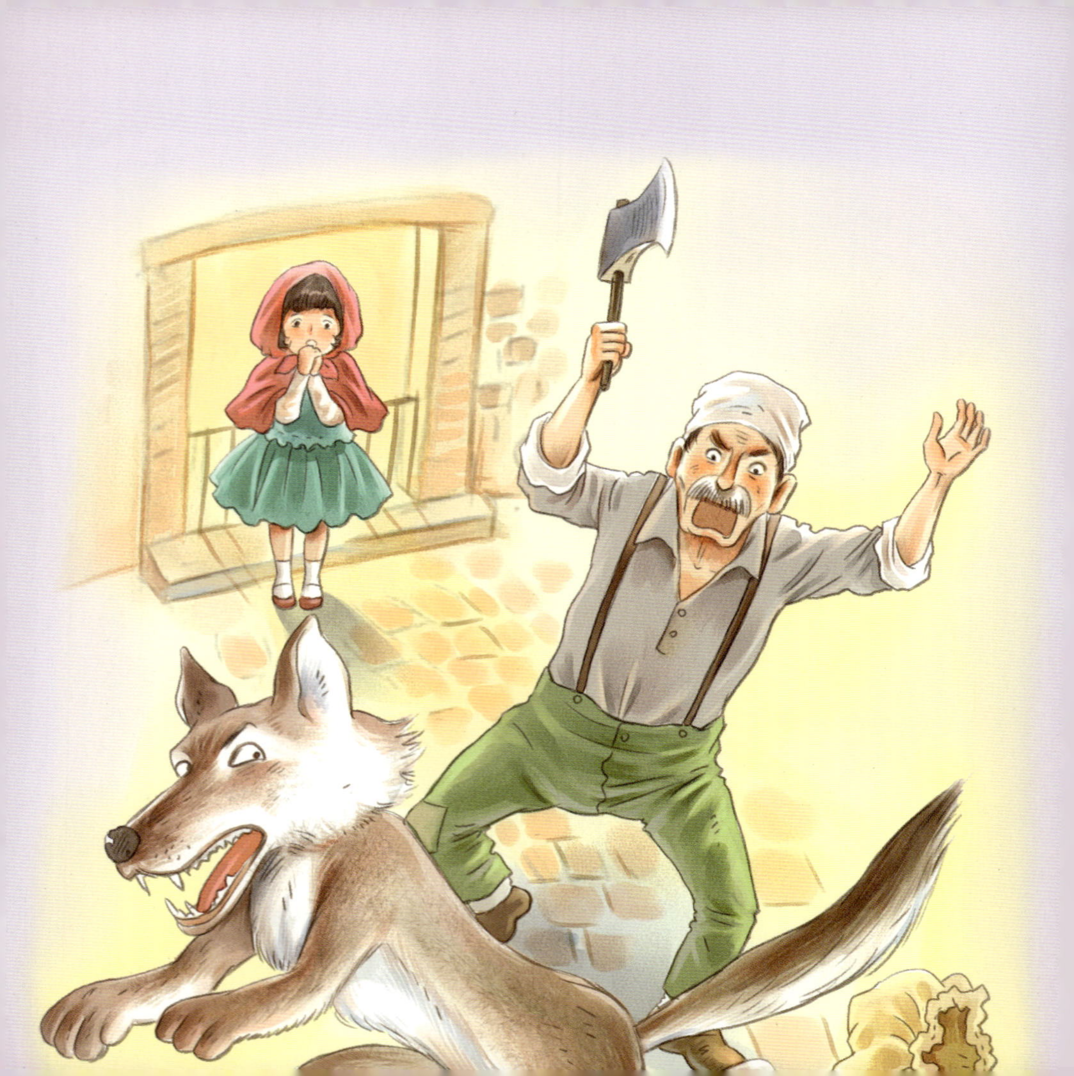

the bed to eat Little Red Riding Hood.

The wolf chased❶ Little Red Riding Hood around the bedroom. "Help! Help!" cried Little Red Riding Hood. "A hungry wolf is trying to eat me!"

A woodcutter heard Little Red Riding Hood and ran to the house. He chased the wolf away with his ax and let Granny out❷ of the basement.

Little Red Riding Hood gave her grandmother a big hug. "I'm so sorry, Granny," she said. "It was all my fault. I told that bad wolf I was coming here. Now, I've learned my lesson.❸ I will never talk to strangers again!"

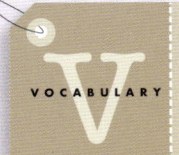

VOCABULARY

1. **chase** v. ☞ ～を追う
2. **let~ out** v. ☞ ～を外に出す
3. **lesson** n. ☞ 教訓

訳：赤ずきん

　昔々、森で母親と暮らす少女がいました。少女の名前は赤ずきんちゃん。

　ある日、母親が赤ずきんちゃんに言いました。
「食べ物が入ったこのかごをおばあさんのところに持っていってちょうだい。家までまっすぐ行くのよ。知らない人と話してはだめよ」

　「約束します」と赤ずきんちゃんは言い、小道を歩き出しました。しばらくすると、1匹のオオカミに会いました。

　「どこへ行くんだい？お嬢ちゃん」とオオカミは聞きました。

　赤ずきんちゃんは約束をすっかり忘れて言いました。
「おばあちゃんの家に行くの！」

　オオカミはすぐ、おばあさんの家へと走りました。オオカミは扉に突進すると、おばあさんを地下に閉じ込めてしまいます。そしておばあさんのパジャマを身につけ、ベッドに入って待ちました。

　間もなく、赤ずきんちゃんが到着します。赤ずきんちゃんはおばあさんの様子がすっかり変わっていることに驚きました。

「なんて大きな目なの、おばあちゃん!」と言いました。

「お前をよく見るためだよ」とオオカミは言いました。

「それから、なんて大きい歯!」

「お前をうまく食べるためだよ!」
オオカミは叫び、赤ずきんちゃんを食べようとベッドを飛び出しました。

オオカミは寝室中、赤ずきんちゃんを追いかけました。
「助けて!助けて!」と赤ずきんちゃんは叫びます。
「お腹をすかせたオオカミが私を食べようとしてるの!」

木こりが赤ずきんちゃんの声を聞きつけ、家に走ってきました。木こりは、斧でオオカミを追い払い、おばあさんを地下から脱出させました。

赤ずきんちゃんは、おばあさんをぎゅっと抱きしめて「ごめんなさい、おばあちゃん」と言いました。
「全部私が悪いの。私があの悪いオオカミに、ここに来ることを言ってしまったの。今、思い知ったわ。もう二度と知らない人と話したりなんかしない!」

Sleeping Beauty
眠れる森の美女

Once upon a time, a king and queen had a precious baby girl. To celebrate,❶ they invited all of their friends and some fairies to a big party.

At the party, each of the fairies were giving the child magical gifts. Suddenly, an evil fairy appeared. "How dare you not invite me!" she shouted. "When this child turns fifteen, she shall prick❷ her finger on a spindle❸ and die!" Then the evil fairy disappeared.

Luckily, one fairy still had a gift to give. "Instead of dying," she said, "the princess will sleep for one hundred years."

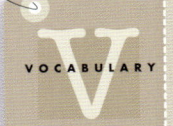

VOCABULARY

1. **celebrate** v. ☞ 祝う
2. **prick** v. ☞ 〜を刺す
3. **spindle** n. ☞ 糸つむぎ

Sleeping Beauty 眠れる森の美女

The princess had no knowledge of the curse as she grew up. On her fifteenth birthday, she discovered a new tower in the castle. She climbed the narrow❶ stairs and saw a dark room. Inside, an old woman sat at a spindle.

The princess didn't know it was the evil fairy! The princess pointed to the spindle. "What is that thing?" she asked as she lightly❷ touched the spindle.

In an instant,❸ the princess fell into a deep sleep. Soon after, everyone else in the castle fell asleep,❹ too. They stayed this way for one hundred years!

VOCABULARY

1. **narrow** adj. ☞ 狭い
2. **lightly** adv. ☞ 軽く
3. **in an instant** ☞ 一瞬のうちに
4. **fall asleep** v. ☞ 眠りに落ちる

Sleeping Beauty 眠れる森の美女

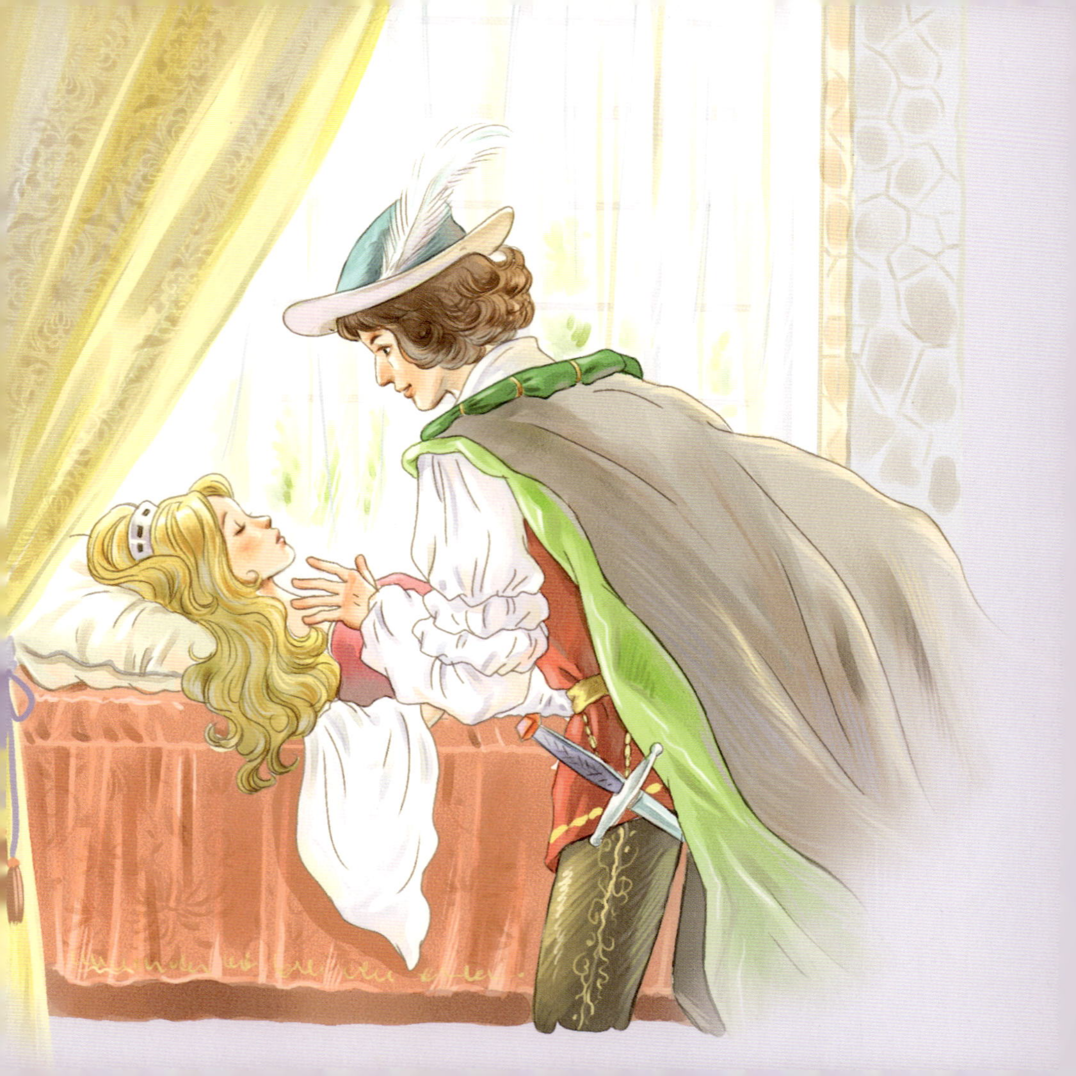

Many years later, a prince was riding his horse❶ in the forest. He came upon the silent castle and was curious.❷ When he went inside, he was surprised that everyone in the castle was asleep.

When the prince reached the top of the tower, he saw the sleeping princess. He thought she was very beautiful. Without thinking, the prince bent down❸ and gave her a kiss. As his lips touched her, Sleeping Beauty opened her eyes and smiled at him.

After this, everyone including the king and queen woke up. The prince and Sleeping Beauty married soon after. They lived happily all of their lives.

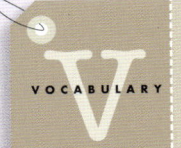

VOCABULARY

1. **ride a horse** v. ☞ 馬に乗る
2. **curious** adj. ☞ 好奇心をそそる
3. **bend down** v. ☞ かがむ

訳：眠れる森の美女

　昔々、王と女王はかわいい女の赤ちゃんを授かりました。お祝いをするため、2人は友人や妖精たちを皆、大きなパーティに招待しました。

　パーティで妖精たちがそれぞれ赤ちゃんに魔法の贈り物をしていると、突然、邪悪な妖精が現れました。
「よくも私を招待しなかったな！」と叫びました。
「この子が15歳になったら、糸つむぎ機に指を挟んで死んでしまうだろう！」そして、邪悪な妖精は消えてしまいました。

　幸運なことに、1人の妖精がまだ贈り物を持っていました。
「亡くなるかわりに、王女は100年眠り続けます」と妖精は言いました。

　王女はこの災難については何も知らずに成長しました。15歳の誕生日、王女は城に新しい塔があるのを発見します。王女は狭い階段を登り、薄暗い部屋を見つけました。中では老婦人が糸つむぎ機の前に座っていました。

　王女はそれが邪悪な妖精とは知りません！王女は糸つむぎ機を指差し、軽く触れながら、

「それは何ですか？」と聞きました。

　あっという間に、王女は深い眠りに落ちました。間もなく城にいるすべての者も眠りに落ちました。彼らは100年もの間、このままだったのです！

　何年も過ぎ、王子が森の中を馬に乗っていると、偶然、静かな城に行き当たります。奇妙に思った王子は中に入り、城の中のすべての人が眠っていることに驚きました。

　塔の上にたどり着くと、王子は眠っている王女を見つけます。とても美しいと思った王子は、何も考えず、かがみ込んでキスをしました。王子の唇が王女に触れると、眠れる美女は目を開け、王子に微笑みました。

　この後、王と女王をはじめ全員が目を覚ましました。王子と眠れる美女は間もなく結婚し、一生幸せに暮らしました。

Beauty and the Beast[1]

美女と野獣

Once upon a time, there was a farmer with three daughters. The youngest daughter was a lovely and kind girl. Her name was Beauty.

One day, the farmer had to go on a journey.❷ He asked his daughters what they would like for a present. Beauty asked only for a rose.

On his journey, the farmer passed a big castle. In the castle's garden, there were some beautiful roses. He went into the garden and picked one. Suddenly, a horrible❸ beast burst out of the bushes.

VOCABULARY

1. **beast** n. ☞ 野獣
2. **go on a journey** v. ☞ 旅に出掛ける
3. **horrible** adj. ☞ 恐ろしい

Beauty and the Beast 美女と野獣

"Please don't kill me," cried the farmer. "The rose was a gift for my daughter. I promised to bring her one from my journey."

"I won't kill you," roared❶ the Beast, "but you must bring your daughter to the castle. She will live with me forever!"❷

At first, Beauty was afraid of the Beast. He was so big and ugly!❸ But slowly she realized he was only a monster on the outside. Inside, he was gentle❹ and nice.

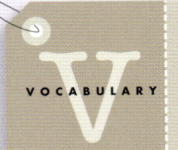

VOCABULARY

1. **roar** v. ☞ ほえる、うなる
2. **forever** adv. ☞ 永久に
3. **ugly** adj. ☞ 醜い
4. **gentle** adj. ☞ 優しい

Then one day, Beauty learned that her father was ill.❶ She begged❷ the Beast to let her go home. "You may go," said the Beast, "but you must return in seven days!"

Beauty went home, and her father quickly got better. Beauty was so happy that she forgot about her promise. Then one night, she saw the Beast in a dream. He was dying of a broken heart!

Beauty ran back to the castle. "Don't die!" she cried to the Beast. "I love you!" Then a miracle❸ happened! Her tears fell on the Beast, and he turned into a handsome prince. Beauty married the prince, and they lived happily ever after.

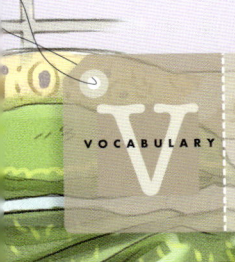

VOCABULARY

1. **ill** adj. ☞ 病気で
2. **beg** v. ☞ 懇願する
3. **miracle** n. ☞ 奇跡

訳：美女と野獣

　昔々、3人の娘をもつ農夫がいました。末の娘は愛らしく心優しい少女でした。娘の名前はビューティ。

　ある日、農夫は旅に出なくてはなりませんでした。農夫は娘たちにプレゼントは何がほしいかと聞きました。ビューティは1本のバラを頼みました。

　旅の途中、農夫は大きな城を通りかかります。城の庭には美しいバラが咲いていました。農夫は庭に入り、1本を摘み取りました。すると突然、醜い野獣、ビーストが茂みの中から姿を現しました。

「どうか私を殺さないでください」農夫は叫びました。
「このバラは私の娘への贈り物なのです。私は旅でバラを1本持ち帰ると約束したのです」

「殺したりしない」ビーストはうなりました。
「だが、お前の娘を城に連れてこい。娘は一生、私と暮らすのだ！」

　始めは、ビューティはビーストを恐れました。ビーストはたいそう大きく醜

かったからです！しかし徐々にビューティは、怪物の姿は外見だけのものであることがわかってきました。その内面は、優しく素晴らしいものでした。

　そんなある日、ビューティは父親が病気であることを知ります。ビューティはビーストに家に帰らせてくれるように頼みました。
「行くがよい」とビーストは言いました。
「だが、7日以内に戻るのだ！」

　ビューティが家に帰ると、父親はすぐによくなりました。ビューティはとてもうれしくなり、約束を忘れてしまいました。そしてある夜、ビューティは夢でビーストを見ます。ビーストは傷心のために死にかけていました。

　ビューティは急いで城に戻りました。
　「死なないで！」
ビューティはビーストに向かって叫びました。
　「愛してるわ！」
すると奇跡が起きました！ビューティの涙がビーストに落ちると、ビーストはハンサムな王子に変身したのです。ビューティは王子と結婚し、2人はずっと幸せに暮らしました。

Cinderella
シンデレラ

There once was a beautiful girl named Cinderella. Cinderella lived with her cruel[1] stepmother and her two selfish[2] stepsisters.[3] They forced her to do all the housework, and they never helped.

Then one night, Cinderella's stepsisters put on their prettiest dresses and went to a royal[4] ball.[5] Poor Cinderella stayed home and cried. She wanted to go so much, but she had nothing pretty to wear.

Suddenly, her fairy godmother appeared. She took out her wand[6] and turned Cinderella's dirty clothes into a beautiful dress. Then she turned a

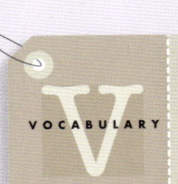

VOCABULARY
1. **cruel** adj. ひどい
2. **selfish** adj. わがまま
3. **stepsister** n. 義姉妹
4. **royal** adj. 王室の
5. **ball** n. 舞踏会
6. **wand** n. 魔法の棒

pumpkin into a golden carriage❶ and six mice into big white horses! Finally, she gave Cinderella a pair of glass slippers.

"Now you may go to the ball," she said to Cinderella. "However, you must leave before midnight. When the clock strikes❷ twelve, the carriage, horses, and your beautiful dress will disappear!"❸

Cinderella was the most beautiful girl at the ball. Her stepsisters didn't even recognize④ her. The prince thought she was a princess and fell in love with her.

Cinderella and the prince danced all night. Suddenly, the clock began

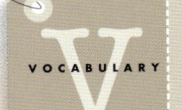

VOCABULARY

1. **carriage** n. 馬車
2. **strike** v.(strike-struck-struck) 打つ
3. **disappear** v. 消える
4. **recognize** v. 気づく

to strike midnight, and Cinderella dashed① out of the castle. She ran so fast that a glass slipper came off② her left foot.

The next day, the prince arrived at Cinderella's house. "A princess left this glass slipper behind,"③ he said. "I want to find her and marry④ her."

The stepsisters tried to squeeze[5] their fat feet into the slipper, but they couldn't do it. Then Cinderella tried it on. It was a perfect fit!

Cinderella and the prince got married and lived happily in the castle. However, her stepsisters weren't happy at all. Now they had to do all the housework themselves.

VOCABULARY

1. **dash** v. ダッシュする
2. **come off** v. 脱げ落ちる
3. **leave~ behind** v. ～を忘れてくる
4. **marry** v. 結婚する
5. **squeeze** v. 押し込む

訳：シンデレラ

　あるところにシンデレラという美しい少女がいました。シンデレラは、意地の悪い継母とわがままな義理の姉妹と暮らしていました。継母と姉妹たちはシンデレラに家事一切を押しつけ、手伝いもしませんでした。

　そしてある夜、シンデレラの姉妹たちはいちばん美しいドレスを着て王室のダンスパーティに出かけました。かわいそうなシンデレラは家で泣いていました。シンデレラは出かけたいのに、着ていく素敵なドレスをもっていないのです。

　すると突然、妖精のゴッドマザーが現れました。魔法の棒を取り出すと、シンデレラの汚い服を美しいドレスに変えました。そしてカボチャを金の馬車に、6匹のネズミを大きな白馬に変えたのです！最後に、シンデレラにガラスの靴を与えました。

　「これでダンスパーティに行けますよ」と妖精はシンデレラに言いました。「でも夜中の12時までには出発しないといけません。時計の針が12時を指したとき、馬車も馬も美しいドレスも消えてしまいます！」

シンデレラは、パーティで最も美しい少女でした。姉妹たちはそれがシンデレラであることに気付きさえしません。王子は、シンデレラを王女と思い、恋に落ちました。

　シンデレラと王子は一晩中踊りました。突然、時計が12時の鐘を打ち始め、シンデレラは城を飛び出しました。あまりに速く走ったのでガラスの靴の片方が脱げてしまいました。

　翌日、王子がシンデレラの家を訪れました。
「王女がガラスの靴をお忘れです」と王子は言いました。
「王女を探し出し、結婚したいのです」

　姉妹たちは、その太い足を靴に無理矢理ねじこもうとしますが、はくことができません。そしてシンデレラがはいてみました。ぴったりです！

　シンデレラと王子は結婚して、城で幸せに暮らしました。一方、姉妹たちはまったく幸せではありませんでした。家事をすべて自分たちでやらなくてはいけなくなったのですから。

The Golden Goose

黄金のガチョウ

Once upon a time, there was a young man named Dummling who ventured into❶ the forest to cut some wood. There, he came across❷ a man dressed all in gray. "Please, sir, can you share some of your food with a hungry old man?" the man asked. "I don't have much food," Dummling replied apologetically,❸ "but what I have I will share."

After eating, the gray man told Dummling to cut down a particular❹ tree. Inside, Dummling found a goose with golden feathers calmly sitting on the roots.❺

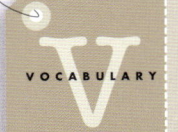

VOCABULARY

1. **venture into** v. ☞ [危険を冒して]〜の中に入る
2. **come across** v. ☞ 〜に遭遇する
3. **apologetically** adv. ☞ 申し訳なさそうに
4. **particular** adj. ☞ 特定の
5. **root** n. ☞ 根元

The Golden Goose 黄金のガチョウ

Delighted, Dummling decided to spend the night at a nearby inn. The innkeeper's three daughters saw the golden goose and wanted one of its feathers. As soon as Dummling left the room, one daughter ran up to take a feather. The moment she touched the goose, however, she found that she could not let go. Her sisters tried to pull her away, but they too became stuck.❶

The next morning, Dummling carried the goose into town, and the innkeeper's daughters had no choice but to follow. Along the way, others tried to help the girls, but they in turn❷ became stuck. Before long, there was a line of townspeople attached to the goose.

Dummling finally came to a large city, which was also the home of the king and his serious daughter. The king had promised the princess's hand in marriage to the first man to bring a smile to her face. When she saw Dummling and the long line of people unwillingly❸ following him, she couldn't help but laugh.

The king did not want a commoner❹ for a son-in-law, so he thought quickly and said, "You must find me a man who can drink the contents❺ of my wine cellar, one who can eat a mountain of bread,

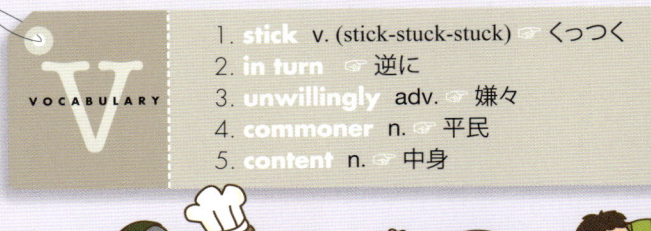

VOCABULARY

1. **stick** v. (stick-stuck-stuck) ☞ くっつく
2. **in turn** ☞ 逆に
3. **unwillingly** adv. ☞ 嫌々
4. **commoner** n. ☞ 平民
5. **content** n. ☞ 中身

and a ship that can sail on both land and water. Only then can you marry my daughter."

Dummling immediately returned to the place where he had met the man in gray and found a man with unquenchable[1] thirst[2] and a man with bottomless hunger. Then the gray man himself appeared and told Dummling he would also give him the ship. "I do all this for you because you were kind to me," the man in gray said.

With the tasks[3] completed, the king reluctantly[4] allowed Dummling to marry his daughter. Dummling lived happily ever after with the princess and never forgot the lesson that kindness can bring surprising rewards.

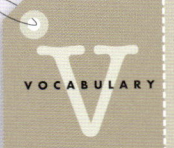

VOCABULARY

1. **unquenchable** adj. 抑えられない
2. **thirst** n. のどの渇き
3. **task** n. 課題
4. **reluctantly** adv. しぶしぶ

訳：黄金のガチョウ

　昔々、森に分け入って木を切るダムリングという若者がいました。ダムリングはそこで全身灰色の着衣をまとった男に遭遇しました。
「お願いだ。この腹をすかせた老人に、食べ物を分けてくれないか？」
と男は頼みました。
「食べ物はあまり持っていないんです」と、ダムリングは申し訳なさそうに答えました。
「でも、僕が持っている分はお分けしましょう」

　食べ終わると、灰色の男はダムリングに、ある1本の木を切るように言いました。木を切ると、ダムリングは、その木の付け根のところに黄金の羽のガチョウが静かに座っているのを見つけました。

　喜んだダムリングは、近くの宿屋で夜を過ごすことにしました。宿屋の主人の3人の娘は黄金のガチョウを見て、羽を1枚ほしがりました。ダムリングが部屋を去ると、1人の娘が羽をとるために駆け寄ります。しかし、ガチョウに触れた途端、娘は動けなくなりました。姉妹たちが引き離そうとしましたが、姉妹たちもくっついてしまいました。

　翌朝、ダムリングはガチョウを町に運びます。宿屋の主人の娘たちはついていくしかありません。道すがら、人々は娘たちを助けようとしますが、逆に、自分たちがくっついてしまいました。やがて、ガチョウに触った町の人々の

長い列ができました。

　ダムリングはついに大きな町に着きました。そこは王とその生真面目な娘の土地でもありました。王は娘を笑顔にした最初の男を娘の夫にすると約束していました。娘は、ダムリングと、心ならずも彼についてきた人々の長い行列を見て、思わず笑ってしまいました。

　王は平民を娘婿にしたくはなかったので、すぐに考えを巡らせて言いました。「君は私のために、私のワインセラーの中のものを飲みほせる男と、山盛りのパンを食べられる男、陸も水もどちらも進める船を探してこなくてはいけない。そうすれば娘と結婚できる」

　ダムリングはすぐ、灰色の男と会った場所に戻ると、抑えられないのどの乾きを抱えた男と、底なしの空腹を抱えた男を見つけました。そして灰色の男が現れ、ダムリングに船も与えると言いました。
「これはすべて、あなたが私に親切にしてくれたからやっているのだよ」と灰色の男は言いました。

　課題をやり遂げると、王はがっかりして、ダムリングに娘と結婚することを許しました。ダムリングはそれからずっと王女と幸せに暮らし、親切が思いがけない褒美をもたらすという教訓を決して忘れることはありませんでした。

The Frog Prince
カエルの王子様

One evening, a princess went outside to play with her golden ball. By accident,[1] she bounced it too high. It bounced over her head and into a nearby pond.[2]

Then, an ugly frog stuck his head out[3] of the water. He said, "I will get your ball for you. But you must promise to love me and to let me live with you!"

The princess just wanted her golden ball back, so she agreed. The frog found the ball and gave it to the princess. She immediately ran home, leaving the sad frog behind.

VOCABULARY

1. **by accident** ☞ 偶然に
2. **pond** n. ☞ 池
3. **stick~ out** v. ☞ 〜を突き出す

The Frog Prince **カエルの王子様**

Later that night, the princess told her father about the frog. Suddenly, she heard a knock❶ at the door. She opened it and was alarmed❷ to see the frog. She slammed the door shut!❸

The princess ran to her father. She said that the ugly frog was at the door. He reminded her that the frog did her a favor.❹ Now, she must keep her promise.

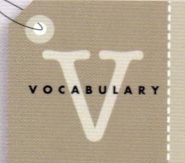

VOCABULARY

1. **knock** n. ☞ ノック
2. **be alarmed** v. ☞ びっくりする
3. **slam a door shut** v. ☞ ドアをバタンと閉める
4. **favor** n. ☞ 親切な行為

The Frog Prince **カエルの王子様**

VOCABULARY

1. **hesitate** v. ☞ ためらう
2. **refuse** v. ☞ 断る、拒む
3. **dine** v. ☞ 食事をする
4. **tongue** n. ☞ 舌
5. **appetite** n. ☞ 食欲

The princess hesitated.❶ Then, she let the frog come inside. She refused❷ to pick him up, though. The frog dined❸ with the princess and her father. The princess watched the frog grab the food with his long tongue.❹ She lost her appetite.❺

The frog thanked the princess for letting him in. Later, the frog asked the princess to kiss him good night. The thought made her sick. She hesitated again. Finally, she closed her eyes and kissed the frog.

To her surprise, the frog turned into a handsome prince! They got married and lived happily ever after.

訳：カエルの王子様

　ある夜、王女は、金の玉で遊ぼうと外に出ました。あやまってボールを高く弾ませてしまうと、ボールは頭の上を越え、近くの池に入ってしまいました。

　すると、醜いカエルが水の中から頭を突き出し、言いました。
「玉をとってあげましょう。でも、僕を愛し、僕と一緒に住むと約束してください！」

　王女は、金の玉を取り戻したい一心で同意しました。カエルは玉を見つけ、王女に渡しました。王女は、悲しげなカエルを残し、すぐに家に走って行ってしまいました。

　その夜遅く、王女は父親にカエルのことを話しました。そのとき、扉をノックする音が聞こえました。王女が扉を開けると、カエルを見つけ、びっくり仰天。王女は扉をバタンと閉めました。

王女は父親のところに駆け寄りました。そして扉のところに醜いカエルがいると言いました。父親は、カエルが王女に親切にしてくれたのだと思い返させます。もう、王女は約束を守るしかありません。

　王女はためらいましたが、カエルを中に招き入れました。ただ、カエルをつかむことは拒絶しました。カエルは王女とその父親と一緒に食事をしました。王女は、カエルが食べ物をその長い舌でペロリとすくって食べるのを見ました。食欲は失せてしまいました。

　カエルは、部屋の中に入れてくれたことを感謝しました。そして、おやすみのキスを王女に頼みました。王女は考えただけで気分が悪くなり、再びためらいましたが、ついに目を閉じ、カエルにキスをしました。

　すると驚いたことに、カエルは見目麗しい王子に変身したのです！２人は結婚し、それからずっと幸せに暮らしました。

The Elves and the Shoemaker

妖精と靴屋

Many years ago, there was a very poor shoemaker. Day after day,[1] he cut patterns out of leather and stitched[2] them together.

One day, business was so bad that he closed his shop early. He left the leather on his workbench and went to bed.

When he woke up the next morning, he saw two pairs of shoes on his workbench. He looked at them carefully. They were perfect.

Later, he sold them to a customer. The customer was impressed[3] by the quality[4] of the shoes. He paid a very high price for them.

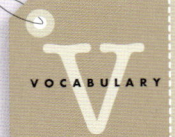

VOCABULARY

1. **day after day** ☞ 来る日も来る日も
2. **stitch** v. ☞ 縫い合わせる
3. **impress** v. ☞ 感心する
4. **quality** n. ☞ 質

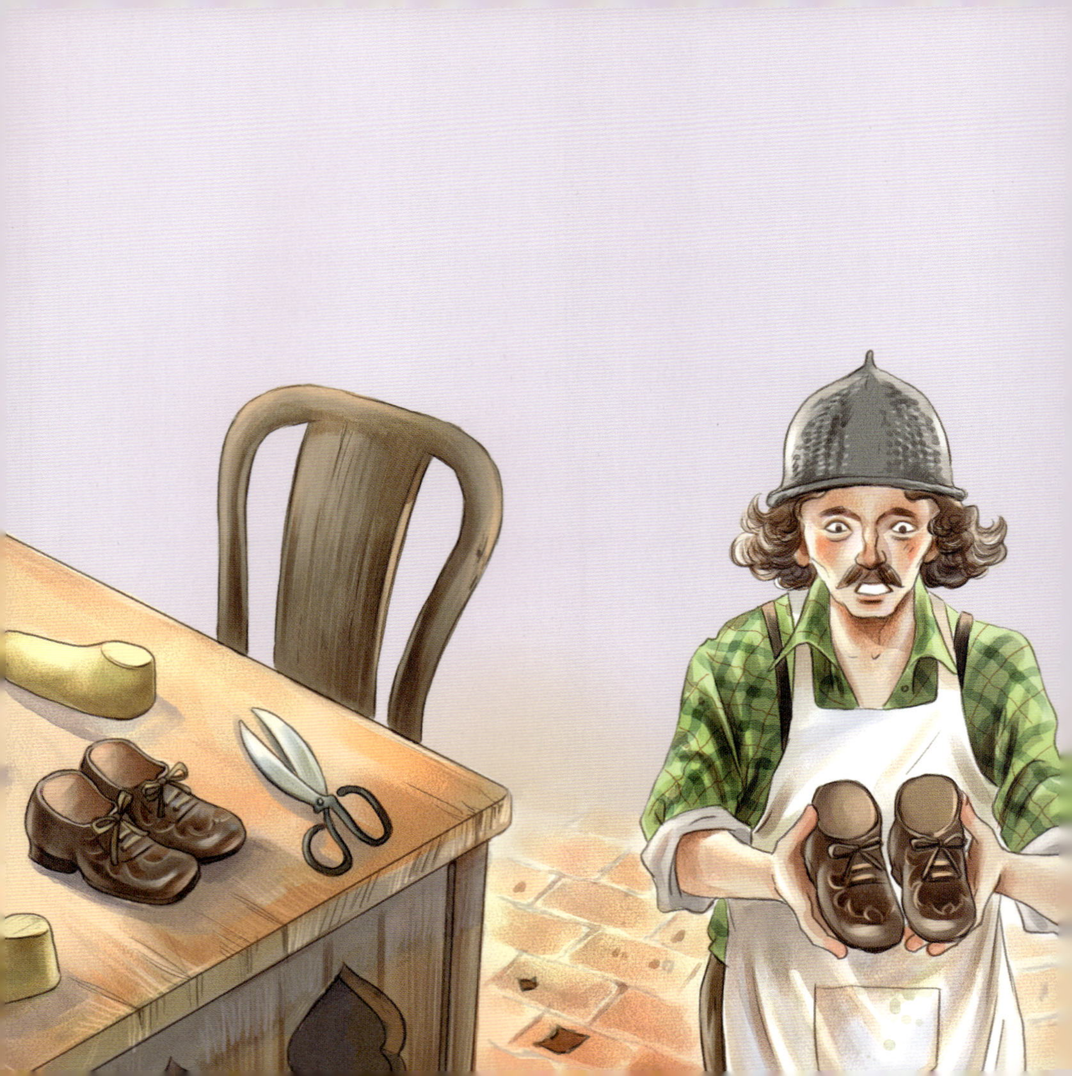

For weeks, the shoemaker would leave leather on the workbench and go to bed. The next morning, he would see new pairs of shoes. Customers loved the shoes. Suddenly, business picked up.❶

One night, the shoemaker closed the shop as usual. However, he hid behind the curtain instead of going to bed. At midnight,❷ two naked❸ elves❹ walked out of the shadows. They picked up some tools and started making shoes. Once they finished, they ran away.

VOCABULARY

1. **pick up** v. ☞ 持ち直す
2. **at midnight** ☞ 真夜中に
3. **naked** adj. ☞ 裸の
4. **elf** n. ☞ 妖精 [複数形：elves]

The next morning, the shoemaker told his wife about the elves. They felt sorry for[1] the naked elves. After all, the elves helped the shoemaker become wealthy.[2]

They thanked the elves by making clothes and shoes in their sizes. That night, the shoemaker left the gifts on the workbench. He stayed up to see their reaction.[3]

The elves were happy and put on their new clothes. Then, they danced out of the shop in their new shoes. This filled the shoemaker with joy.

VOCABULARY

1. **feel sorry for** v. ☞ 〜を気の毒に思う
2. **wealthy** adj. ☞ 裕福な
3. **reaction** n. ☞ 反応

The Elves and the Shoemaker **妖精と靴屋** | 109

訳：妖精と靴屋

　昔々、とても貧しい靴屋がいました。来る日も来る日も、革を型紙通りに切っては、それらを縫い合わせていました。ある日、仕事もなく早々に店じまいをした靴屋は、作業台の上に革を置いたまま、ベッドに入ってしまいました。

　翌朝起きると、靴屋は作業台の上に2足の靴があるのを見つけます。靴屋はじっくりとそれらを眺めましたが、完璧な出来でした。

　その後、靴屋はその2足の靴をお客に売りました。お客は靴の質の高さに感激し、たくさんお金を払ってくれました。

　数週間、靴屋は作業台の上に革を置いて寝ることにしました。翌朝には新しい2足の靴があるのです。お客はみな靴をとても気に入りました。にわかに仕事は上向きになります。

ある夜、靴屋はいつものように店を閉めました。でも、ベッドに入らずにカーテンの陰に隠れていました。深夜、暗闇から２人の裸の妖精が出てきて道具を手にとると、靴を作り始めました。仕上げるとすぐ、妖精たちは走っていなくなってしまいました。

　翌朝、靴屋は妻に妖精たちのことを話しました。夫婦は裸の妖精たちがかわいそうになりました。妖精たちは靴屋が豊かになるように助けてくれていたのです。

　夫婦は、妖精たちに感謝するために、妖精のサイズの服と靴を作りました。その夜、靴屋は作業台に贈り物を置いておき、彼らの反応を見るために起きていました。

　妖精たちは喜んで新品の服を身にまといました。そして、新品の靴をはいて店の外に出て踊りました。これを見て、靴屋は喜びで一杯になったのでした。

Clever Gretel
賢い
グレーテル

One day, Mr. Peterson told his cook, Gretel, that a guest was coming over. He wanted her to roast[1] two hens[2] for them, so Gretel put two hens over a fire.

After a while, the hens turned brown. But Mr. Peterson's guest hadn't arrived yet. Gretel noticed that one of the wings was burning. "What a shame,"[3] she said. She ate the wing so that it wouldn't burn anymore.

A few hours went by. Mr. Peterson's guest still hadn't arrived. She couldn't even find Mr. Peterson. "Perhaps they went somewhere else for dinner," Gretel said.

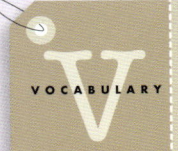

VOCABULARY

1. **roast** v. ☞ あぶり焼きにする
2. **hen** n. ☞ めんどり
3. **what a shame** ☞ もったいない

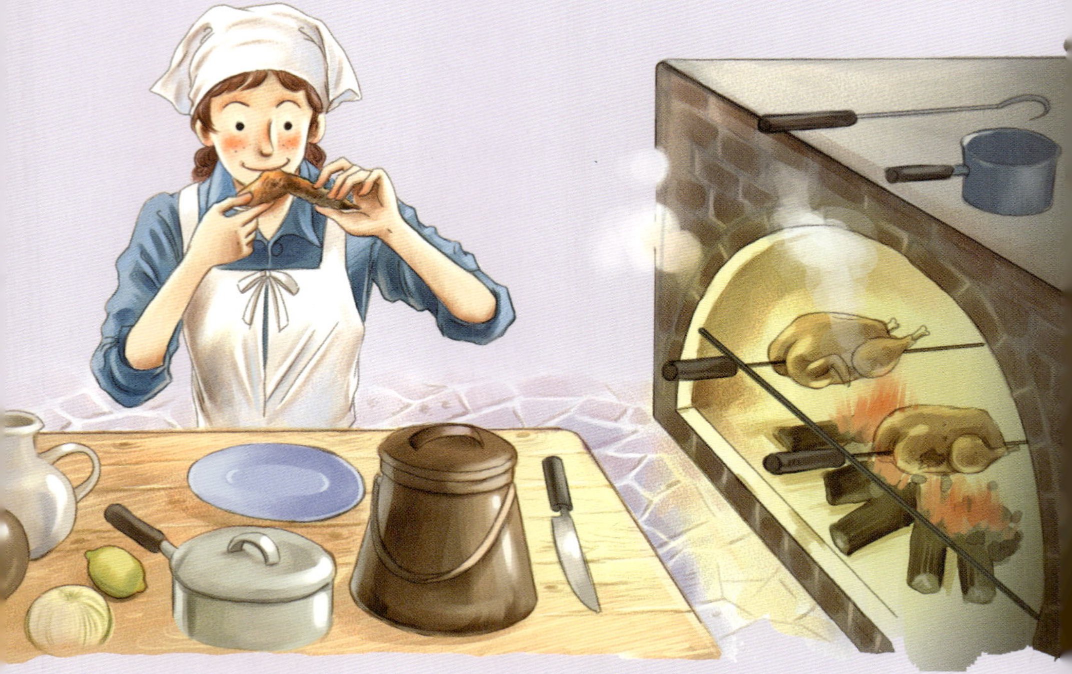

"Well, I've already started eating one of the hens," she said. "I might as well[1] finish it." Gretel ate the rest of it. It was so delicious that she ate the second hen, too.

Suddenly, Gretel heard Mr. Peterson's voice. "My guest is here! Let him in!" Mr. Peterson ran to the dining room table and picked up a knife. He was hungry for a hen.

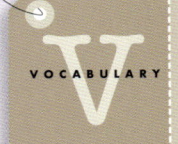

VOCABULARY

1. **might as well** ☞ 〜した方がいい

VOCABULARY

1. **whisper** v. ささやく
2. **yell** v. 叫ぶ

Gretel ran to the front door. She whispered❶ to the guest, "You must leave! Mr. Peterson wants to cut off your ears!" This scared the guest, and he started running away.

Then, Gretel went into the dining room and said, "Mr. Peterson, your guest just ran away with both hens!" Mr. Peterson ran after him, but he forgot to put down the knife.

Waving the knife in the air, Mr. Peterson yelled,❷ "I just want a hen!" But the guest was covering his ears with his hands. Meanwhile, clever Gretel went to bed with a full stomach.

訳：賢いグレーテル

　ある日、ピーターソンさんは、料理人のグレーテルに、来客があることを伝えました。めんどりを2羽焼いてほしいというので、グレーテルは2羽のめんどりを火にかけました。

　しばらくすると、めんどりがこんがりキツネ色になってきました。でも、ピーターソンさんの客人はまだ到着していません。グレーテルは翼の片方が焦げてきているのに気付きました。
「なんてことでしょう」
そう言ってもう焦げることが無いように、翼を食べてしまいました。

　さらに、数時間が過ぎました。ピーターソンさんの客人はまだ来ません。ピーターソンさんの姿さえ見当たりません。
「2人はきっとどこかに夕食に行ったのだわ」
とグレーテルは言いました。

「そうね、もうすでにめんどりを1羽食べ始めてしまったし」とグレーテル。
「全部食べ切ったほうがいいわね」と、グレーテルは残りも食べてしまいました。とてもおいしかったので、グレーテルはもう1羽のめんどりも食べてしまいました。

すると突然、グレーテルはピーターソンさんの声を耳にしました。
「お客様がいらしたよ！出迎えてくれ！」
ピーターソンさんは食堂のテーブルにかけてきてナイフを取り上げました。めんどりが食べたくてしかたがなかったのです。

　グレーテルは玄関に走って行き、客人にささやきました。
「立ち去ったほうがいいですよ。ピーターソンさんは、あなたの耳を切り取ろうとしています！」
これを聞いて客人はこわくなり、逃げ出してしまいました。

　次にグレーテルはダイニングに入っていき、言いました。
「ピーターソンさん、お客様は２匹のめんどりと一緒に、たった今逃げて行きましたよ！」
ピーターソンさんは客を追いかけましたが、ナイフを置いてくるのを忘れていました。

　ナイフを振り回しながら、ピーターソンさんが叫びます。
「ただめんどりがほしいだけなんだ！」
しかし客人は両手で両耳をふさいでいます。この間に賢いグレーテルは満腹になってベッドに入りました。

Lucky Hans
幸運なハンス

Hans was a lighthearted[1] boy. When he quit working for his master, he was paid some silver coins. He decided to take them home to his mother. On his way, Hans met a man with a cow.

"Those coins look heavy!" the man said. "Coins can't walk by themselves, but a cow can. Why don't we trade?"[2]

VOCABULARY

1. **lighthearted** adj. ☞ のん気な
2. **trade** v. ☞ 交換する

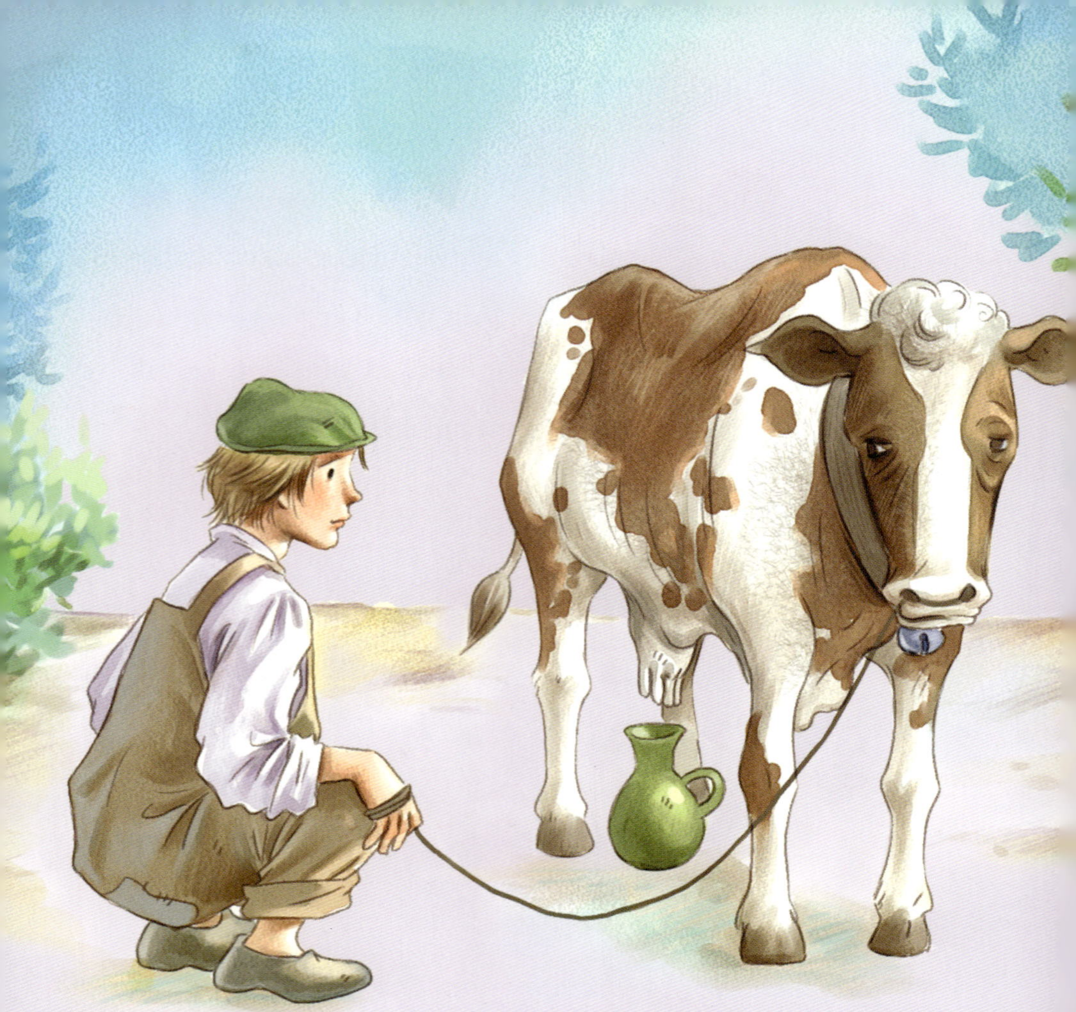

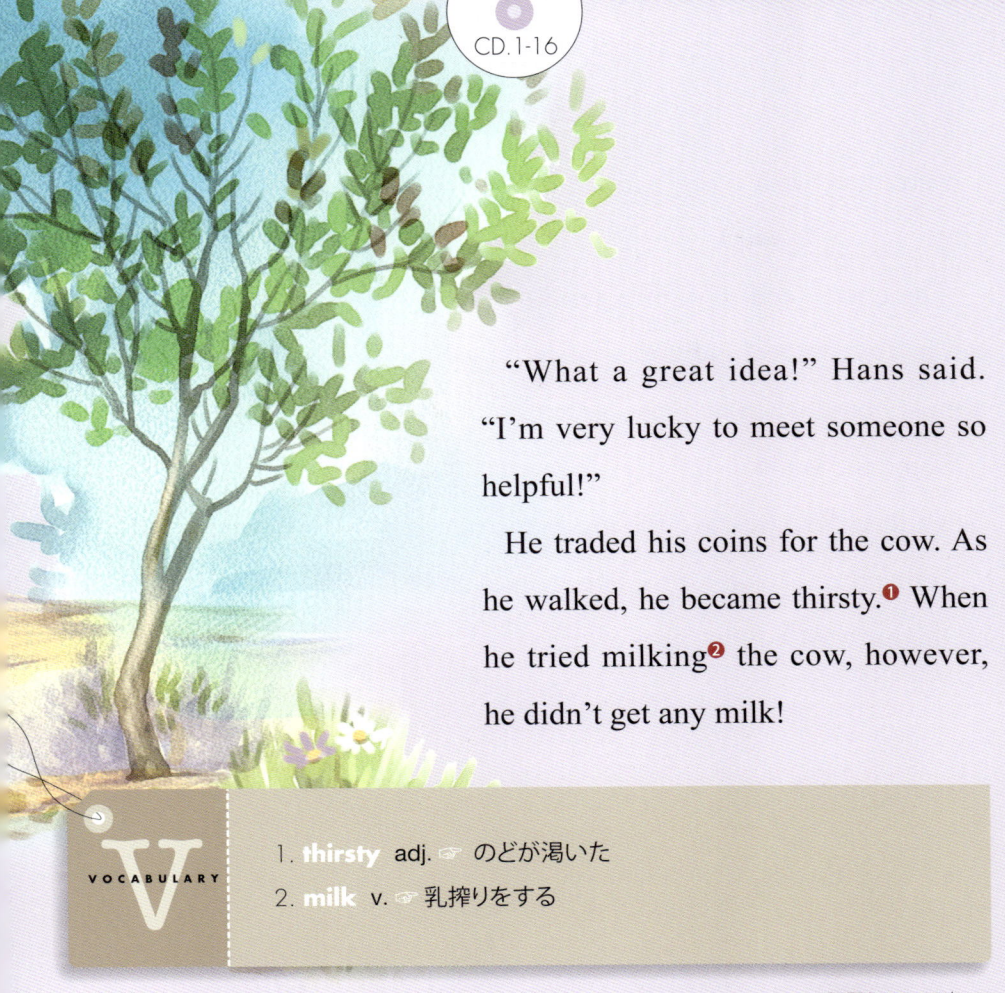

"What a great idea!" Hans said. "I'm very lucky to meet someone so helpful!"

He traded his coins for the cow. As he walked, he became thirsty.❶ When he tried milking❷ the cow, however, he didn't get any milk!

VOCABULARY

1. **thirsty** adj. ☞ のどが渇いた
2. **milk** v. ☞ 乳搾りをする

A stranger with a pig walked by❶ and saw Hans trying to milk the cow.

"The cow is old. It's only good for beef," he said. Hans hated beef, but he loved pork! He traded his cow for the stranger's pig. Hans was almost home when he met another man.

"Someone is stealing❷ pigs," the man said. Hans didn't want to look like a thief,❸ so he gave the pig to the man and went home.

"Whenever I have a problem, someone helps me!" he said. "I must be the luckiest boy in the world!"

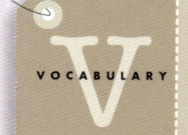

VOCABULARY

1. **walk by** v. ☞ 通りかかる
2. **steal** v. (steal-stole-stolen) ☞ 盗み取る
3. **thief** n. ☞ 泥棒

Lucky Hans **幸運な**ハンス

訳：幸運なハンス

　ハンスはのん気な少年でした。主人のもとで働くのをやめたとき、ハンスはいくらかの銀貨をもらいました。ハンスは銀貨を家にいる母に渡すことにしました。その途中、ハンスは牛を連れた男に会いました。

「その銀貨は重そうだな！」と男は言いました。
「銀貨は自分では歩けないが、牛は歩ける。交換しないかい？」

「なんてすばらしいアイディアなんだ！」とハンスは言いました。
「こんなに僕を助けてくれる人に会えるなんて僕は果報者だ！」

　ハンスは銀貨を牛と交換しました。歩いていると、ハンスはのどが渇いてきました。牛の乳を絞ろうとしますが、乳は少しも出ません！

豚を連れた見知らぬ人が通りかかり、牛の乳搾りをしているハンスを見ました。

「その牛は年寄りだ。肉にしか適さないよ」とその男は言いました。
ハンスは牛肉が嫌いでしたが、豚肉は大好き！ハンスは牛をその男の豚と交換しました。もうすぐ家に着くというとき、ハンスは別の男に出会いました。

「誰かに豚を盗まれてしまった」と男は言いました。
ハンスは泥棒のように見られたくなかったので、その男に豚を与え、家に帰りました。

「問題が起きるといつも誰かが僕を助けてくれるんだ！」とハンスは言いました。
「僕は世界でいちばん幸運な少年に違いない！」

Index

索引

A

afford	33
apologetically	89
appetite	100
at first sight	35
at midnight	107
attract	27
awful	53

B

ball	81
bargain with	9
basement	58
be alarmed	98
beast	73
beg	77
bend down	69
blind	37
bray	34
bread crumb	17
break off	18
burst through	58
bush	37
by accident	97

C

capture	34
carriage	83
celebrate	65
chase	61
cheer	27
chop off	34
claim	13
club	37
coal	37
coffin	53
come across	89
come in	18
come off	85
come upon	18
commoner	91
complain	41
content	91
crow	34
cruel	81
curious	69

D

dare	37

dash	85
day after day	105
desert	37
dine	100
disappear	83
disappointed	9
divide	9
drown	11
dutifully	41
dwarf	51

E
elf	107
encourage	41

F
fair	49
fall asleep	66
fall into	37
fault	28
favor	98
fee	28
feel sorry for	108
forever	75

G
gentle	75
get rid of	9
give birth to	49
go on a journey	73
(be) good at ~	25
goodness	49
granny	58

H
handsome	35
hen	113
hesitate	100
horrible	73
housework	18
hundreds of	25

I
ill	77
immediately	35
impress	105
in an instant	66
in secret	28
in turn	91

K
knock	98

L
lead	28
lean into	21

leave ~ behind	85
lesson	61
let ~ out	61
light	21
lighthearted	121
lightly	66
live happily ever after	21
live in the woods	56

M

marry	85
mean	17
meanwhile	11
meow	34
might as well	115
milk	123
miracle	77
mourn	53

N

naked	107
narrow	66
nearby	33

O

ogre	11
out of pity	51

P

pajamas	58
particular	89
path	56
peddler	51
pick up	107
pond	97
possession	9
prick	65
punish	33

Q

quality	105

R

reaction	108
recognize	83
refuse	100
reluctantly	93
ride a horse	69
roar	75
roast	113
rob	11
root	89
royal	81
run away	41

S

scream	37
selfish	81
servant	51
set eyes on	53
set off	41
slam a door shut	98
spindle	65
squeeze	85
stab	37
stand up to	17
steal	124
stepmother	21
stepsister	81
stick	91
stick ~ out	97
stitch	105
stranger	25
strike	83
succeed	25

T

talent	13
task	93
thief	124
thirst	93
thirsty	123
threaten	11
tongue	100
townspeople	25
trade	121
turn ~ into	13

U

ugly	75
unquenchable	93
unwillingly	91

V

venture into	89

W

walk by	124
wand	81
wander	51
wealth	13
wealthy	108
what a shame	113
whisper	116
witch	18
with great sorrow	53
woodcutter	17

Y

yell	116

LiveABC

　株式会社 Live ABC は、台湾の e-Learning プログラムにおいてトップレベルの実績を誇っている大手出版社です。最先端の IT 技術と経験豊富な技術者と語学教師及び編集スタッフによって、インタラクティブマルチメディア語学学習教材の研究開発に取り組んでいます。
　現在、英語を筆頭に中国語、日本語、韓国語などの語学学習教材を、書籍や、CD-ROM、スマートフォン対応のアプリで提供しています。

ホームページ（英語）： http://www.liveabc.com

カバーデザイン	土岐 晋二（d-fractal）
本文デザイン／DTP	土岐 晋二（d-fractal）
英文翻訳	佐藤 淳子
CD ナレーション	Jack Merluzzi
	Carolyn Miller
	城内 美登理

音読 CD BOOK ④
やさしい英語で読む　グリム童話　～ Grimm's Fairy Tales ～　BEST 15
平成 23 年（2011年）　8月10日発売　初版第1刷発行
令和 元 年（2019年）　12月10日発売　　第2刷発行
編　者　Live ABC
発行人　福田富与
発行所　有限会社　J リサーチ出版
　　　　〒166-0002　東京都杉並区高円寺北 2-29-14-705
　　　　電話 03 (6808) 8801（代）FAX 03 (5364) 5310
　　　　編集部 03 (6808) 8806
　　　　http://www.jresearch.co.jp
印刷所　（株）シナノ パブリッシング プレス

ISBN978-4-86392-070-5　禁無断転載。なお、乱丁・落丁はお取り替えいたします。
Copyright ©2011 LiveABC Interactive Corporation
Japanese translation copyright ©2011 J-Research Press. Japanese edition. All Rights Reserved.